Trading Closets: Out of Darkness and Into His Marvelous Light

REVISED EDITION
By Crystal D. Jenkins

Published by Crystal Dawn Jenkins
Hampton, VA

Trading Closets: Out of Darkness and Into His Marvelous Light
Revised Edition
ISBN – 978-0-615-99127-6
LCCN - 2014916251
Copyright © 2014 by Crystal Dawn Jenkins
All publishing rights belong exclusively to Crystal Dawn Jenkins

Cover Design – Mona Jenise, Dream Designs Graphics, http://www.dreamdesignsgraphics.com

Printed in the United States of America.

Acknowledgements

*This revised edition of Trading Closets is dedicated to my maternal grandmother, **Estelle P. Mitchell**. Your love for God, faith and perseverance will always encourage me to trust the Lord in all I do and never quit!*

I love you grandma.

Table of Contents

Forward

Trading Closets by Crystal Jenkins is a breath of fresh air in a world of conflicts and compromises concerning sexuality. Readers will find this book exposes one into the psyche of men and women struggling with the complex issues of gender identity. Today the reasonable explanations that appeal to our human consciousness range from the proverbial to the colloquial phrases of *"I was born this way and have always felt I was a man in a woman's body or vice versa"* to *"I have always had a natural attraction to the person of the same sex"*. As our world continues to erase the standards of our design as men and women within the laws of nature Crystal enables us to see that God cares and can deliver any individual if one is willing to release, forgive and apply the universal truth given to us all.

The truth of Genesis 1:27, which says, "So God created man in his own image, in the image of God created he him; male and female created he them." The truth of the words of King David found in Psalm 139:14, ' "I will praise You, for I am fearfully *and* wonderfully made; Marvelous are Your works, And *that* my soul knows very well." The truth of John 3:16, "For God so loved the world that he gave his only Son, for whoever believes in him will have everlasting life." This is a life eternal both everlasting and a kingdom quality of life that is of God where we are able to experience the holistic peace of heaven on earth as we relate to each other as sexual beings without the compromise.

Trading Closest enables all of us to experience the power of transformation when one receives the love of God regardless of social and economic demography. God's love is for everyone but there are choices everyone must make to walk in the fullness of His love. This book enables us to see the process and impact of those choices. As a result, there are some moments where many will have to prepare and dress for life and in order to do so they will have *to come out of and trade closets* to be who they really are.

Dr. Ray Johnson,
Pastor, Calvary Revival Church - Peninsula

It's time for the church to be rightly related to all its children. Crystal's open life in *Trading Closets* will help others find love, truth and freedom.

Rev. Janeen L. McBath,
Co-Pastor, Calvary Revival Church - Norfolk

Stage One:
From FEAR to FAITH

"Be alert and of sober mind. Your enemy the devil prowls around like a roaring lion looking for someone to devour. Resist him, standing firm in the faith..."

(1 Peter 5:8-9, NIV)

~ 1 ~
Portrait

I'm sitting in the classroom. My teacher, standing in front of the class, announces it is time to take our weekly test. I will never forget this day. Her hair is neatly lying on her shoulders. Her button-down white shirt is as crisp as the morning air, and her brown twill skirt is flowing like the ocean. As she walks by my desk, a strange feeling comes over me. My mind begins to race. What is this? Why are these thoughts impeding my mind? I must be dreaming. Not me. No, no, no. Silence. At this moment, I knew something was happening to me. Boys had never given me *this* tingling sensation. Could it be true?

Experiencing same sex attraction at such an early age was overwhelming. I was a child and did not know what I was experiencing. I enjoyed being around girls more than boys. I'd rather play with cars than dolls. I wanted to play outside instead of staying inside. Was this a bad thing? It was not until middle school that I began to realize what I was experiencing. My peers talked about and taunted the "gay" students. I even joined in sometimes. I quickly learned it was to my benefit to be a part of the "in crowd." As long as I didn't share my secret, I could avoid the same ridicule.

Unsurprisingly, I encountered a similar situation at home. My family embraced a strong Christian faith. My mother made sure we were in church every Sunday. If I didn't know about anyone else, I knew about Jesus Christ. I recall my family speaking negatively about "gays" whenever they would see something about them on television. I vividly remember being scared stiff as a two-by-four when I was in the room with my family. I always thought that my body language would reveal that unlike them I would enjoy whatever was on the television. I did not want my actions to disclose my secret. It was as if they could read my mind if I even so much as moved, so staying still kept me safe. The last thing I needed them to know was that their baby girl was a closet lesbian.

I became saturated in brokenness and shame. Homosexuality was blasphemous in our home. No matter how hard I tried, I could never bring myself to expose my secret. I did not know how to share my innermost thoughts. I became so discouraged and frustrated that I completely shut everyone out of my life. I isolated myself. My self-esteem was non-existent and I did not care about anything or anyone.

I began drinking and smoking. I often thought about running away and committing suicide. The years seemed to pass slowly, so I had to keep busy to feel sane. Maintaining good grades kept me occupied. I was also in a long distance relationship with a young man during high school. However, when he graduated we parted ways. All I remember is counting the days until my high school graduation. I would be a step closer to finally being free to be myself.

Graduation arrived and I was on my way to college. As a college freshman, I attempted to find myself because I was convinced God made me this way. I was finally able to be the tomboy I was comfortable being...or so I thought. Even though I was comfortable on the outside, I was still on edge inside. My fears eventually consumed my life and had not only forced me into a shell, but had also forced me to accept my life as a "nobody." I was consumed with 'approval addiction,' which author and speaker Joyce Meyer simply defines as the need to please everyone. I was constantly seeking approval from my peers. I lived my life to please everyone around me, eventually realizing I did not love myself. I felt hopeless and sought something to fill the void in my life. Alcohol became my daily resource to sooth my worries and fears.

Even through my college matriculation, God kept me. I was not out of the closet because so many people from my hometown attended the same college. I dated a few young men to "fit in" with my friends, but I never changed my style as a tomboy. I decided they could accept me as I was or just not date me. In my mind, this rationale supported that I was a lesbian at heart. Later, in my junior year, I reconnected with my high school sweetheart and we married about three years later. I hoped our union would bury my homosexual feelings forever.

Almost four years into my marriage, I began experiencing same-sex attraction again. I thought I had defeated this struggle, but I realized this was a stronghold in my life. I was becoming attracted to co-workers, married women and strangers I met online. I prayed about what was happening in my life. I eventually told my husband about my feelings. My hope was this could open the door to healing and reconciliation. Instead, this gave the enemy bargaining power. Neither of us was in a position to deal with the bondage of homosexuality over my life or in our marriage. Our faith was not strong enough. Promiscuous thoughts eventually plagued our relationship and ultimately ended our marriage.

Later that same year, I had my first homosexual encounter with a former roommate. There was no initial attraction, but as we began spending more time together an attraction developed. Totally opposite from me, my first girlfriend was a tall, athletically-built, extremely feminine woman who wore four inch heels almost every day. She definitely portrayed the *femme* role, which is the person who takes a traditionally feminine role in a homosexual relationship. I, on the other hand, portrayed the soft stud (or butch) role as the more dominant, masculine person in the relationship. As I began making my transition, she would often go with me to get my hair braided. It was after one of those nights that we embarked upon the beginning of our relationship.

After this initial experience, I believed this was truly the life for me. I was a proud stud, but full of fear! No more dresses, no more heels, no more purses. I could finally rock my jeans, tees and cornrows. Immediately, I felt the desire to finally come out to my family and friends. Their reactions were expected. My family temporarily abandoned me, and a few good friends left forever. It was all good. My life had changed. I was happy and free. Nothing else mattered.

My first partner and I moved in together after only a few months. Even though I was happy and in love with my partner, I was convicted daily. I did not understand. I was consumed with the battle between my lifestyle and my livelihood. I was struggling spiritually and confused. How could God make me this way but I still feel so guilty?

After less than a year, I became depressed because my relationship with my partner was failing. We were arguing almost daily and it was not healthy for the household. I became so distraught; thoughts of suicide crossed my mind often. I remember it so clearly. We were getting ready for work when I locked myself in the bedroom. My partner knew I had a knife and some pills in the room and I told her I was going to end my life. She immediately called the police. When I realized they were in another area of the apartment, I tried to get myself together and convince them I was just joking. Once they entered the room, it was obvious I needed help so I was taken to the hospital. Thankfully, I had not ingested enough pills to do myself serious harm. I was placed in an evaluation room with security posted outside my door. God kept me.

What I did not know is that my partner had also called my mother. When I saw my parents enter my hospital room, my heart stopped. I was full of anger and embarrassment. I did not want anyone, especially my parents, to see me this way. My life as I knew it was over. I lied and convinced my parents my issues were related more too financial difficulty and depression. They already didn't approve of my lifestyle, so I didn't want to make it any worse for myself.

On my own recognizance, I sought professional, Christian counseling. I received the recommendation from my pastor at the time. In each session, my counselor would say the same thing week after week. "Crystal, your struggle with lesbianism all revolves around one question: "Will you choose His life or your life?"" My answer was always the same. "One day, I know I will choose His life, but right now I am not there yet." As each week went by, I toiled with the decision of my life or God's life. I decided I would not date, hoping this would help me clear my mind.

Well, not dating didn't last long at all! Within a month after my last session, I met another local woman online. In less than a week, we met in person. I am not a firm believer in love at first sight, but we had an instant emotional connection. We had a great relationship, lasting for over three years. Even after I engaged in a short-lived affair our second summer, we were able to reconcile. I knew I had found the woman God had for me. Unlike my previous partners, this woman was not out of the closet. We did not let that stop our right to love one another. We did everything together. We took vacations, visited amusement parks, went on picnics and attended church together. Yes, this woman too had a relationship with Jesus Christ. Now I was convinced my life as a lesbian was acceptable. I had met someone who loved Jesus just as much as I did.

I was finally at a point in my life where things were beginning to settle down and my peace was returning. Happiness and love were in the air and I was beginning to work on my relationship with God. He [God] and I were finally on the same page. So that God and I could have a fresh start, I decided to seek out a new church home. I wanted to be able to worship as a lesbian and not worry about people gossiping about me. I researched several churches online that accepted homosexuals, but my partner was never keen on attending any of these. So I ended up just randomly visiting churches Sunday after Sunday.

One particular Sunday, I overslept and was running too late to attend the church I had found for that week, so I got in my car and headed towards downtown in my city. There was a church on every other block so eventually I just randomly selected a church. Upon entering, they were still collecting the offering, so I just took a seat in the back.

Shortly thereafter, the pastor was introduced and I realized I knew him from my previous church. There was a sense of disgust in my spirit because I didn't want to see anyone I knew. Immediately, I got up to walk out but I could feel the Holy Spirit saying "sit down," so I ended up staying the entire service. Not only was I blessed by the Word, but I felt a tug in my spirit like I was home. I remember chuckling to myself saying "God, you surely have a sense of humor." God had led me to the one church I did not want to attend because I would once again be around familiar people. But even in the midst of my lifestyle, I knew to obey the Holy Spirit.

On my third visit to the church, the pastor was speaking on a general announcement when all I heard was "As long as I am alive, in this city marriage will be between one man and one woman!" There was a thunderous shout after his statement, and for the first time in years I felt convicted about my lifestyle. I remember rushing home, calling my partner and explaining what happened. I was so emphatic that I remember her advising me to calm down several times. I didn't know whether to be angry or relieved about his statement or what I felt inside. After sharing what happened, I recall the phone line being very quiet. So I asked my partner what was wrong. She began to cry and said "C.J., I have been feeling that way for a while now but I was afraid to tell you." I was *numb*.

Over the next few months, my partner's spiritual life began overcoming her flesh. She was becoming more involved in her church and kept encouraging me to attend services with her. It seemed like every conversation we had mentioned God and how our life was not pleasing Him. Our quality time was cut in half and our intimacy became non-existent. The more that conversation came up, the more I was internally convicted, but I was determined to be hard core and not waiver from my position. She constantly reminded me that our families would not be pleased, and that was a personal risk she was not willing to take. More than anything, my girlfriend told me over and over and over again that no matter how much she loved me, the thought of living an eternal life in hell terrified her and that alone was enough to make her leave the life.

This same thought began to permeate my spirit. I, too, realized that hell was not an option for my life after death. Over time, my inner spirit [the Holy Spirit] began defeating my outer spirit [my flesh] and I was beginning to truly desire freedom and deliverance. Who would know that her renewed spirituality would ultimately end our lesbian relationship and begin the restoration of our spiritual purpose.

~ 2 ~
Transition

D ay in and day out, I cried "Oh Lord, when will it be over? Will I ever be delivered? Will I ever be free?" I wondered if He could even hear my cry. I lived each day in fear. All I wanted to do was end my life so the pain would be over.

It was hard enough being a woman. It was even more difficult to keep up a Christian façade so no one knew the ugly truth about my life. I was an emotionally-scarred stud trapped in a Christian body. Each day when I looked into the mirror, I had hoped to see the reflection of a beautiful mural filled with love and happiness. Instead, I saw nothing but a blemish covered in hurt and shame.

It would not be until months later that I realized this was a part of God's plan for our lives. My partner used to always tell me that our spiritual purposes were not being fulfilled by being in a relationship together. She was insistent that our relationship was blocking our blessings. Eventually, I decided to seek spiritual guidance from my pastors. I was at a crossroads in my life, and did not know which way to go. My heart was guiding me to the left and my spirit was guiding me to the right.

So who better to talk to than my pastors who were emphatic that God's word makes it clear homosexuality is not of Him. I loved and respected my pastors, so I was open to their counsel. I was very honest in our sessions, disclosing my past and my present. We discussed everything from what I thought the source could have been and to how it was affecting my current day-to-day life. My pastors were very understanding and non-judgmental, but serious about what the word of God said. The most vivid thought I was left with was *"I could not allow my past to determine my future because God has greater plans for me. But until I was ready to let my flesh go and truly live in purpose, I would be like a slave to my lifestyle."*

I honestly remember saying I was about 80% free... like that was a good thing. What I have come to know, however, is that anything less than 100% sold out to God just does not cut it. Like the song says 99 and a half just won't do. I had always believed that with prayer and surrendering faith, my life could be changed. And not to my surprise, his counsel confirmed that my lifestyle decision was not of God and the only person standing between me and deliverance was the woman in the mirror.

It was not until I made the personal decision to seek God and draw nearer that I began to feel a change. During our annual time of consecration, I submitted my whole being to God. I wanted to be delivered and set free from homosexuality. When that day finally came, all I could feel was relief. Tears streamed down my face, chills ran through my body, and the precious Blood of Jesus Christ cloaked my once-dead spirit.

On January 5, 2012, while praying in my own home, my deliverance process began! I declared unto God that I was ready to take my life back from the enemy. In the most powerful yet assuring voice He said, "My child, through your obedience comes freedom." I was tired of being in bondage and not walking in the will of God. My faith was nearly dead, but thank God my release had already been orchestrated. ""For I know the plans I have for you," declares the Lord, "plans to prosper you and not to harm you, plans to give you hope and a future."" (Jeremiah 29:11, NIV). Despite the enemy's many schemes to kill me emotionally, spiritually and physically, God had a different plan. There was a sweet peace in my spirit. I was ready to embrace my freedom.

What am I to do now? How do I approach this walk into a life free from homosexuality? How do I leave the closet that had me bound? For twenty-five years I struggled with homosexuality, but my day of freedom has come. "Therefore submit to God. Resist the devil and he will flee from you. Draw near to God and He will draw near to you..." (James 4:7-8).

You see, freedom is a process. This book was birthed months before my first lesbian encounter, but it was not finished until I had endured my wilderness and transitioned into my purpose. Even after my prayer of deliverance, I struggled with my flesh for almost another year. I found myself arguing and fighting with people from my past life. The enemy was clever because these arguments were not over me having an attraction to women. I had dealt with that demon, so the enemy had to find another weakness in my life: my insecurities.

One argument in particular involved my most recent former girlfriend being interested in a young man. When I found out he had been to visit her, I became infuriated. I was angry because God had opened a door for her and not for me. I had been praying for God to bring a man into my life but it had not happened. I felt betrayed because by this time, two of my prior girlfriends were married to men. The enemy had convinced me that a relationship with a man was not in the cards for me. Not only was this a bold-faced lie, it opened the insecurity wounds in my flesh and I began feeling betrayed. When I confronted her, I blamed her for not being a real friend and for leaving me alone. I even began to feel like it was easier when we were together. Oh the enemy thought he had me because I was tempted to go back. This particular argument escalated into threats being made and before we realized it, a knife had been pulled and each of our lives was in danger. Thankfully, no one was hurt that night and since then God has restored our broken friendship. And so it is clear: the only relationship with a man that is 100% necessary is a personal relationship with Jesus Christ!

I share this to show that the devil does not want to see you free or happy, so he will tempt you in any and every way to send you back to a life that leads to a burning hell. You see, I prayed for deliverance and God moved. However, I still had to deal with my flesh. We have to take full responsibility for our own actions and that includes our flesh. I had to constantly speak death to my flesh. I had to expressly speak that my flesh was dead to homosexuality.

About a year and a half after my prayer of deliverance, my flesh died and it was yet another exhilarating experience. This time was even more profound in Him because now I have no desire, no temptation, and no set-backs! I am free and my newness in Christ has begun! Partial freedom is no freedom at all. There is nothing like total freedom in Jesus Christ.

God knows the purpose for your life and He will guide you through the transition. Make the decision in your heart, trust Him, be obedient to His word and watch your life change!

~ 3 ~
Trading Closets

I have come to realize that my life as a lesbian was a closeted affair. I was always hiding from someone; therefore, I was never 100% honest with who I was. Do you know who you are?

As is known to many, until you decide to be public with your sexuality you are considered *in the closet*. Here, you form your identity and you decide how you will live your life. There is a problem though, because during this process you are alone. The atmosphere is full of confusion, destruction and doubt. What many don't realize is that you never fully come out of this closet. Why? No one can fully come out of something that becomes unknown territory. You do not know what to expect when you come out. This unknown expectation keeps you bound forever whether you admit it or not.

Well, it is your time. You are officially "out of the closet." You prepare to enter society not knowing how you will be perceived or if you will be accepted. You are confident in who you are outside of the closet. Life feels natural. Why, then, do you still have an inner gut feeling of insecurity?

I was in the closet for almost twenty years. When I finally began living my life as a stud, I experienced an internal conflict. I never fully escaped my initial closet. I was careful not to reveal my sexuality to my colleagues because of the industry in which I worked. When I attended church, I never wore a skirt or a dress, but I would dress as to camouflage myself in the crowd. And even when I went to visit my family, it was made clear I would not disrespect them in how I presented myself.

Outside of all the nuisances in my life, I thought I was finally free. I mean I laughed. I smiled. I was me. Life was great. I had a good job, met some really nice friends, began dating, attended church and had no real complaints. My only regret during this time was why it took me so long to come out. I felt like I had missed out on life and was trying to make it all up at once. So this was it. This was my life. Free at last.

Wait. Why is it that life seems all good, but I still feel empty inside? Why is it that I have the time of my life when I'm out, but when I get home I feel alone? I am out! I am free! I am finally being me! Why do I feel so uneasy inside? What am I missing? The real question was *WHO* am I missing?

So did I really come out of the closet? Or was I just in the wrong closet? It was at this point in my life when I knew it was time to trade closets. Are you at that point in your life where you are ready to make the personal decision to reclaim your identity? Are you seeking a new life?

It is your time to completely come out of the closet that holds darkness, loneliness and no guidance in life. Trade closets. There is no confusion, only answers. There is no darkness, only light. Loneliness does not exist because Jesus is always there. Enter your spiritual closet. Embrace peace, comfort and the best part of all: a new friend.

Jesus welcomes your company, for in your spiritual closet you embrace open communication with the Father. You can enjoy quiet time with your new best friend and begin understanding your transition. Your new identity is revealed and the stronghold of homosexuality is broken. Your purpose is being defined, and the entrapment is over. Your healing process can begin. Are you ready? It is time to find your renewed spirituality. It is time to trade closets.

My purpose in writing this book is to help other women overcome the stronghold of homosexuality. Some people experience instantaneous deliverance from strongholds. My life experiences have shown me that total liberation from the spirit of homosexuality will be an ongoing process. No single day is easy, but each day I embrace that I am not who I used to be. I am new in Jesus Christ. I am a beautiful woman and I love me! "Therefore, if anyone is in Christ, he is a new creation; old things have passed away; behold, all things have become new" (2 Corinthians 5:17).

Open your heart to receive God's Word as you walk through the next four critical stages of healing and deliverance. I thank God in advance for total freedom as He heals others with a similar portrait to my own.

Reflections

Recall the time when you first identified with homosexuality. Paint your portrait.

_____

_____

_____

_____

_____

_____

_____

_____

_____

_____

_____

_____

_____

~ 4 ~
The Spirit of Fear

Y ou should never fear your life. Grab your boxing gloves and step into the ring! Fear cripples you mentally and physically. If you are not careful, it will take full control of your life. Do not allow fear of people knowing about your struggle to keep you in bondage. You will learn that people will always have something to say about you whether good or bad. Don't suffer from approval addiction because it will stifle your spiritual growth. The spirit of fear has the power to convince you that life is better off a secret. You will begin to think it is easier to cover up than to come out. Do not give way to this trick of the enemy.

Fear as a noun is derived from the Old English word 'faer,' which means danger or peril. God does not operate in fear—nor should we—for the scripture teaches, "For God has not given us a spirit of fear, but of power and of love and of a sound mind" (2 Timothy 1:7). For over twenty years, I lived in fear of who I had become. Actually, I lived in fear of who I thought I had become. Know who you are in Christ. Know your identity.

Homosexuality was not my only struggle. I was also addicted to (and unable to accept, uncover, or reveal my struggle with) alcohol. What was I doing claiming to be a child of God but full of deceit, guilt, and shame? I say that to say this: coming out of fear and bondage is not an easy or necessarily a short process; however, there is nothing greater than the peace you receive when the battle is over. What you must remember is that even with awesome and loving people in your life, you cannot be free from your fears until YOU make the decision to walk with God and be set free. You must start by surrendering your every thought and action to God. Start small and win big.

Understand the mind is a very powerful muscle. It is indeed the first place the enemy attacks. This muscle exercises 24-7. One major setback is the belief you have control of the mind. The truth is, the only thing you can control is what you feed into it. You cannot control how it reacts. Think about the death sentence you would put on yourself if you had control over how the mind responded. Honestly, how can you control the mind which you cannot see, when keeping your flesh under control is a daily battle? Be mindful that the enemy's gift is entrapping your mind and making you feel depressed, lonely and valueless. Learn to beat him at his own game. Protect your mind.

Constant feelings of worthlessness and humiliation all stem from various situations, some untold, that haunt thousands of women daily. The enemy attacks the mind first because if he can control your mind, he knows he can control you. Therefore, it is imperative to guard your mind. Understand that God can and will free your captive mind if you surrender to Him. You must not succumb to the spirit of fear but overcome with a spirit of faith. You cannot be afraid of what could be. God does not fail. No matter whom you are—single or married, young or old—you do not have to live in fear. Your past does not have to define your future. You may look at your life and say "Yes, I was afraid." Some of you may be saying "Yes, I *am* afraid." Know there is no need to feel ashamed or embarrassed. Expose the enemy and let him know he has no more power over your life. Let him know you have no fear because the Lord our God has made you victorious!

God has all power and He is not a selfish God. He has already given you that same power and self-control. Your responsibility is to believe and have faith. I do not want to sound like a broken record but this is important. He makes life so easy for us but we sit here and complicate it daily. Satan has already been defeated. "Behold! I have given you authority and power to trample upon serpents and scorpions, and [physical and mental strength and ability] over all the power that the enemy [possesses]; nothing shall in any way harm you" (Luke 10:19, AMP). Learn to fight each attempt the devil makes to gain leverage in your life by simply defeating him with the name of Jesus.

Even though your mind may be held captive by emotional distress, remember who ultimately has all control. If you are living in fear right now, know that God has already delivered you from the hand of the enemy. "Do not conform to the pattern of this world, but be transformed by the renewing of your mind. Then you will be able to test and approve what God's will is—His good, pleasing and perfect will" (Romans 12:2, NIV).

When you make the decision to be free from the lifestyle, your victory party begins. Learn to rejoice with each small triumph as you prepare for the grand celebration. If you are reading this book then you have already won the first mental battle over the enemy. The victory party continues! You are a conqueror and not a casualty. The Scripture promises us that, "Yet in all these things we are more than conquerors through Him who loved us. For I am persuaded that neither death nor life, nor angels nor principalities nor powers, nor things present nor things to come, nor height nor depth, nor any other created thing, shall be able to separate us from the love of God which is in Christ Jesus our Lord" (Romans 8:37-39). Isn't it refreshing to know nothing can separate you from the love of God? You do not just win the battle but you overwhelmingly defeat the enemy. Start your fight today.

You cannot confront what you do not identify, and you cannot conquer what you do not confront. The identification has been made. No fearful situation is too great for God. There is no scar God cannot erase. There is no wound God cannot mend. Celebrate God daily and allow Him to feel your gratefulness for the small. In Matthew 25:23, His word promises if you are faithful over the small things, He will make you ruler over the big things. Step in the ring, confront your fear and with God you will overcome!

Reflections

Identify your fears. How does each prevent you from confronting your sexual identity crisis?

_____

_____

_____

_____

_____

_____

_____

_____

_____

_____

_____

_____

_____

_____

_____

How important is making the decision to take this journey into freedom to you?

_____

_____

_____

_____

_____

_____

_____

_____

_____

_____

_____

_____

_____

_____

_____

~ 5 ~
If You Believe

G od loves you just the way you are. In fact, He loves you so much that He made the ultimate sacrifice with His own Son. "For God so loved the world that He gave His only begotten Son, that whoever believes in Him shall not perish, but have eternal life" (John 3:16). Can you imagine the love God has for you if He willingly gave His ONLY child to die so you could live? Even if no one has ever loved you, find joy knowing God loves you the same yesterday, today and tomorrow. "But God demonstrates His own love toward us, in that while we were still sinners, Christ died for us" (Romans 5:8).

Just think, you mean so much to God that even in the midst of living a sinful life, He stills loves you. Can you ask for anything better? This supernatural, unselfish, and unconditional love that Jesus Christ has for you is like no other. He is the sweetest name we know, and just from His love alone, you are a new person in Him. God's love surpasses any love you may think you can receive. His love exceeds that from any mother, any father, any man, any woman, any addiction or anything else you may substitute for love. You may feel filthy or impure but He loves in spite of.

Please, take this opportunity right now to speak to yourself and declare that, "Jesus loves me." Say it with excitement and conviction, "Jesus loves me!" Now say it and believe it: "Jesus loves me...despite all my issues, despite my past, despite my right now, despite my hurt and pain, Jesus loves me! Out of all the people in this world, JESUS LOVES ME!" I feel a rush in just writing this! You know that warm feeling you are experiencing right now; that's the presence of God. Know if no one else does, your Heavenly Father loves you!

God loves you so much that He has already equipped each of us with a measure of faith. The Bible even compares that measure to a grain of mustard seed. "If you have faith as small as a mustard seed, you can say to this mulberry tree, 'Be uprooted and planted in the sea,' and it will obey you" (Luke 17:6, NIV). Our responsibility is to believe and see ourselves healed in the future *right now*. In other words, have the healed mentality even in your time of distress. Activate your faith and your fear will obey you.

Faith is like the muscles in your body. If you go to the gym for thirty minutes daily then you build strength in your heart. This routine helps maintain a healthy body. You must do the same thing with your faith. On a daily basis, you must find time to spend with God so you can become one with Him constantly exercising your faith. This helps maintain a healthy spirit. Exercise your faith daily. Bathe yourself in His presence. Feel His loving arms hold you close to His heart and celebrate life knowing you are free in Jesus Christ. We need to constantly be filled with the presence of the Lord. Ephesians 3:16-19 reads:

"16 that He would grant you, according to the riches of His glory, to be strengthened with might through His Spirit in the inner man, 17 that Christ may dwell in your hearts through faith; that you, being rooted and grounded in love, 18 may be able to comprehend with all the saints what is the width and length and depth and height- 19 to know the love of Christ which passes knowledge; that you may be filled with all the fullness of God."

Rest with reassurance that by faith, if we open our hearts to receive Him, He will fill us with His fullness. God has given you the power to overcome. Exercise your faith and begin to walk in the Spirit. Trust God; He will never let you down.

Think about this. You take chances for everything else in life, so why not try God. When you become a woman of faith and embrace the friend that is God, life's problems will automatically begin to straighten out. During this process, you will find yourself enjoying His presence and no longer focusing on the problem. Remember: God has already given us the victory. Be patient and rest in the Lord. Have F-A-I-T-H and freely accept God's intimate, true healing. Make up your mind and profess, "I have chosen the way of faithfulness; I have set my heart on your laws." (Psalm 119:30, NIV). With each new day, you have just won another battle.

Exhale. Count your victories. Breathe the fresh breath of life.

Reflections

In what areas of your life do you trust God to heal and begin your freedom process?

_____

_____

_____

_____

_____

_____

_____

_____

_____

_____

_____

_____

_____

_____

What can you begin doing to increase your faith in God?
How will you make this a daily commitment?

_____

_____

_____

_____

_____

_____

_____

_____

_____

_____

_____

_____

_____

Journal

Use the next few pages as a personal journal. Write down your thoughts and feelings. Reflect on how you felt before and after reading Stage One.

_____

_____

_____

_____

_____

_____

_____

_____

_____

_____

_____

_____

_____

Stage Two: From Repression to Revelation

"I will extol You, O LORD, for You have lifted me up, And have not let my enemies rejoice over me. O LORD my God, I cried to You for help, and You healed me... You have turned for me my mourning into dancing... That my soul may sing praise to You and not be silent. O LORD my God, I will give thanks to You forever."

(Psalm 30:1-2, 11a-12; NASB)

~ 6 ~
Breathe Again

Are you living a life that looks pleasing on the outside, but inside you are dying? Why are you repressing your innermost thoughts and feelings? There is a lack of willingness to openly communicate about what is inside. Is it not enough you fear your life? Do not fear confessing your struggles. This does not necessarily mean to tell the world. Talk to God. Break the routine of repression; stop pretending the pain will just go away. Be encouraged right now to bind that repressive feeling in the name of Jesus.

According to Merriam-Webster, *repression* means to hold in by self-control or to exclude from consciousness. When you make the conscious decision [an act of self-control] to hold in your life, you repress it to your unconscious being. So when you think about it, you actually exert more mental and physical energy in repressing your sentiments versus dealing with them at the forefront.

Let me paint another picture for you. Being bound by repression is like sentencing yourself to life in prison with the possibility of parole after forty years. You wake up in captivity, unable to break the chains which bind your mind. You spend the entire day drowning in frustration and shame unable to see beyond the dark walls of your experiences. You go to bed each night unable to shake the shackles that strain your heart.

With good behavior and your faith, you receive the reward of temporary freedom. Now you have permission to go outside for a breath of fresh air, and you finally begin to realize that this temporary break is only giving you back what used to be yours anyway. Yet because you failed to obey the law [Word of God], you are now confined behind barbed wire and an electric fence, constantly reminded of your past. Immediately, you realize that this so-called freedom is nothing more than a forged memento of your present reality. Will you live this false reality and possibly wander in the wilderness for forty years like the Israelites? Or will you make the decision to be obedient to God's Word and instantaneously be set free? Cry out to the Lord saying, "Bring my soul out of prison, so that I may give thanks to Your name; the righteous will surround me, for You will deal bountifully with me" (Psalm 142:7, NASB).

Learning to be open and honest requires trust. Trusting people is difficult, but trusting God is oh so easy. Ask Him for guidance and He will provide it. Become a woman after God's own heart. Be obedient to His Word and you will be a step closer to a new life in Jesus Christ. Some never get a second chance. You do! Release your troubles, failures and shame, your unyielding past or your existing situation. Obedience is the key to freedom. Will you walk in obedience and accept His invitation? Will you trust in Him and finally breathe again?

Now is the time that you can openly accept Jesus Christ as your personal savior.

Say this simple prayer:

"Dear Jesus, thank You for loving me so much that You gave Your life for me. I want a new life and relationship with God, My Father. I believe You died on the cross and rose again. Come into my heart and forgive me of all my sins. Heal my wounds and help me breathe again. Thank You for this new life. In Jesus' name, Amen."

Praise God you are now saved! Welcome to the Kingdom!

Reflections

Reflect on areas in your life you have repressed. Why do you think you are afraid to share these experiences?

_____

_____

_____

_____

_____

_____

_____

_____

_____

_____

_____

_____

_____

_____

_____

Who or what is in control of your life right now? What can you do to take your life back and become the woman God has destined you to be?

_____

_____

_____

_____

_____

_____

_____

_____

_____

_____

_____

_____

_____

_____

~ 7 ~
God's Divine Truth

H ave you ever heard the saying "You are what you eat?" Well in life, you can also become what you experience. Therefore, do not let your negative experiences determine the road in life you will travel.

Let me share how God revealed His divine truth in my life. My childhood experience sculpted the beginning of my adult life. My mind had become poisoned by the sexual images I had seen on television so many times. These images were ingrained in my thought life and over time influenced my perception of women and the attraction I felt towards them.

As time progressed, I realized I did not know how to freely give or receive affection. The enemy used this against me. I began to feel uncomfortable when I was around women, and I honestly thought it was immoral to show affection towards another woman unless I had a valid reason. But what was considered valid? I struggled becoming close to a woman without thinking there was an attraction. Even when genuine friendships developed,

I was always questioning my feelings on whether there was an attraction or not. My thoughts made me feel corrupt and sinful. Therefore, not only was I a disappointment to myself, but I knew God was not happy.

How many of you feel the same way? You love the Lord, but you have some dark secrets that hinder your relationship with Him. Guess what? He already knows and still loves you the same! God has blessed you with the free gift of revelation. Now, whether you receive this gift is up to you. You see, revelation simply means God makes known His divine truth. Therefore, God has blessed us all to receive His divine truth. And what is truth? Truth is *God's Word*.

God's Word cannot be changed or destroyed and remains unconditionally consistent. The only change factor is you. Will you read the Word? Will you study the Word? Spending time in God's Word must become a daily routine. It should become something that you yearn to do each and every day. Days will come when you are tired, weary, frustrated and even doubtful, but through it all you must stay in the Word. If for no other reason, the Word provides peace of mind and gives you victory over the enemy. The enemy can do nothing about God's divine truth. It is complete. He may try to distract you or tempt you to believe otherwise, but hold on to God's Word. He promises, "So will My word be which goes forth from My mouth; it will not return to Me empty, without accomplishing what I desire, and without succeeding *in the matter* for which I sent it" (Isaiah 55:11, NASB). If you listen and adhere to His word, His plan is always fulfilled.

Make the decision to walk in a divine relationship with God and experience a new revelation. Each and every day strive to "...walk in a manner worthy of the God who calls you into His own kingdom and glory" (1 Thessalonians 2:12, NASB). You must make the conscious effort to give God your all. Make Him FIRST. Find time to spend with Him and He will comfort you each day in joy and peace. "For you will go out with joy and be led forth with peace..." (Isaiah 55:12, NASB).

As I began to grow in God, I learned to accept His divine truth. He revealed through His word I was neither an alcoholic nor a homosexual. I am the daughter of the King; I am royal priesthood; I am free. "So if the Son makes you free, you will be free indeed" (John 8:36, NASB). The same is true for you. Do not believe the lies that the enemy places in your mind. Open your spiritual eyes and your true identity will be revealed. As you begin spending more time in His presence, you will discover you can love women you care for without having an unhealthy physical attraction.

What better friend have we than Jesus! One who knows our hearts, our souls, our innermost thoughts, and still time after time again, He gives us the opportunity to know Him more intimately. Thank God for the gift of revelation. Truly, there is nothing greater than His divine and awesome truth. "The Spirit of the Lord GOD is upon me, because the LORD has anointed me to bring good news to the afflicted; he has sent me to bind up the brokenhearted, to proclaim liberty to captives and freedom to prisoners..." (Isaiah 61:1, NASB). Exhale. You are healed. You are free.

Reflections

At this moment, your life represents a combination of your past & present. It is time to finally be honest with whom you really are. What "lies" are you living?

_____

_____

_____

_____

_____

_____

_____

_____

_____

_____

_____

_____

_____

_____

Now disprove each "lie" by reflecting on God's revelation in your life. What truths has He promised you?

_____

_____

_____

_____

_____

_____

_____

_____

_____

_____

_____

_____

_____

_____

_____

Journal

Use the next few pages as a personal journal. Write down your thoughts and feelings. Reflect on how you felt before and after reading Stage Two.

_____

_____

_____

_____

_____

_____

_____

_____

_____

_____

_____

_____

_____

_____

Stage Three:
From GUILTY to GUILT-FREE

"How blessed is he whose transgression is forgiven... when I kept silent about my sin, my body wasted away through my groaning all day long... I acknowledged my sin to You, and my iniquity I did not hide; I said, "I will confess my transgressions to the LORD"; and You forgave the guilt of my sin"

(Psalm 32:1-5, NASB)

~ 8 ~
Learning to Forgive

"Thank God I'm healed, but why do I feel so guilty?" Many people can be healed from homosexuality, infirmities, addictions, situations and circumstances but remain with a sense of guilt, shame and condemnation. People who have been offended or experienced deep hurt have a difficult time forgiving, but forgiveness is essential to have a pure heart and open line of communication with God. Be careful not to nurse old wounds. Walk in forgiveness, not revengefulness.

For example, imagine your neighbor accidentally backs into your car which is parked on the street. When he informs you, you are understandably upset, but since the damage is just a few scratches it is ok. Now, as a good neighbor would, he agrees to pay for any repairs. He asks for your forgiveness and you agree. This is how God's Word teaches us to handle these situations. At this point, if we genuinely forgave our neighbor there would be no more issues.

However, many do not stop here. You have allowed this incident to develop into a grudge you are now holding against your neighbor. You go into the house and gossip with your best friend about how your neighbor is so careless. Your negativity is now penetrating your spirit and you begin speculating that the accident was on purpose. Perhaps you even go to the point of saying you hope someone hits his car one day. Well, less than a month later, you find out your neighbor was involved in a serious car accident that claimed his life. You immediately feel guilty for the grudge you had against him all this time. See, the grudge was unknown to the neighbor, but it has eaten at the core of your spirit and now as a result you feel guilty about his death even though you played no role.

Now this ending is dramatic, but think about the many times in your life when you had the opportunity to forgive but instead you left someone emotionally scarred. We must be careful that we consistently walk in genuine forgiveness and not allow the grudges in life to permeate our spirit. God forgives us more than we can keep record and never looks back. We must learn to forgive others in the same way. "For if you forgive others for their transgressions, your heavenly Father will also forgive you. But if you do not forgive others, then your Father will not forgive your transgressions" (Matthew 6:14-15, NASB).

A lack of forgiveness will haunt your spirit. You cannot fully enjoy the benefits of God's healing if you continue to hold grudges. Forgiveness should be genuine and from your heart, not just from your lips. When you offer forgiveness with the wrong attitude or intention it becomes what I call "watered-down."

For example, you are assigned to work on a team project. You and your partner contribute equal effort to complete the project on time and therefore receive excellent reviews. However, during the evaluation process your partner takes full credit saying you did not contribute. Later he comes to you explaining that he needed to impress the manager because he is up for a promotion and asked for your understanding and forgiveness. You remind him that it is not good business practice to lie but you will forgive him. As time progresses, you make the conscious decision to not communicate with or work with your partner. When he asks why, you remind him of the incident and share that you are still offended. Your working relationship is now strained. Our very human nature can lead us to walk in un-forgiveness. Follow the heart.

Like repression, prison can also symbolize the lack of forgiveness. With daily repentance, you walk in freedom; without it, you wander in the wilderness. We all will encounter a wilderness season, but how long is determined by our faith walk. Follow self, maximum sentence; follow God, instantaneous grace and mercy. "There is a way that appears to be right, but in the end it leads to death" (Proverbs 14:12, NIV). Without walking in forgiveness, freedom will be unattainable. It is a crucial part of your healing process. Remember: through obedience comes freedom. Fully submit to God; letting go of all past and present hurts, pains and offenses. Ask

God to help you forgive those you have hurt you. Yearn to forgive; yearn to be free.

Un-forgiveness traps you in a never-ending cycle of self-pity and shame. You cannot move forward. Imagine someone holding a dirty rag against you. The filth will always be connected to you. Over time it takes power over you. You lose sight of everything God has for you. But once you learn to walk away [forgive], the rag falls aside. The grudge is released by God. You are no longer controlled by the situation, but God is now in control of your destiny.

In no way am I saying it will be easy. It has taken me years to forgive certain people in my life. And it is not about them necessarily knowing you must forgive them. It is all about you getting *you* right and *you* standing right before God. Open your heart, recharge your faith, and the forgiveness process will openly flow.

Now let's be honest. Everyone has faith, whether confessed or not. How many people examine a chair before they sit down? Not many. Think about it. Have you ever seen a person at a restaurant pick up the chair and make sure the legs are tight and all the screws are secure before they sit down to enjoy dinner? Probably not and why; because whether they accept it or not, they exercise faith and believe that the chair is properly assembled and safe to use. So what happens when you do check things out around you? This time of in-between faith occurs when you enter a place in life where you must decide which way to go. You have faith in God and believe His Word, but at the same time you doubt what will happen as a result of a situation you are facing.

Where do you stand on your faith scale? Most likely you are in-between. I would even dare to say the majority of our lives we are probably at a place of in-between faith. This place in our walk with God is absolutely necessary. Without it, the greatest thing about being in a place of in-between faith would not be revealed. During your in-between faith season, God not only shows up but He receives all the glory from your story. The more you depend on Him, God moves on your behalf and everyone around you will know God is who He says He is.

So, how do you transition from in-between faith? How do you choose the right path? This can be done in three simple steps. Yes, just three steps! **First, pray.** Talk to God about what you are facing. This is your time to open up and share your deepest thoughts and not have to worry about <u>anyone</u> else knowing. God is the ultimate best friend. "Do not be anxious about anything, but in every situation, by prayer and petition, with thanksgiving, present your requests to God. And the peace of God, which transcends all understanding, will guard your hearts and your minds in Christ Jesus." (Philippians 4:6-7, NIV).

Second, listen. Take the time to listen to God when He is speaking. It is easy to get caught up in making your petitions known to Him without realizing the direction He may be trying to communicate to you. Often times, you can pray and ask for God's help, but then keep doing what you were doing before you prayed. You must learn to just stop and listen. Sit down. Be still. Some of the best time in God's presence is during quiet time. As many of my teachers used to say, why do you think you have two ears and just one mouth? Even in God's splendid creation of man, He designed us to listen more than we speak.

Third, obey. Whether you like what God says to your spirit or not, obey. He may not always direct us to the easy path; however, you must know He will always guide you toward the right path. "Commit your way to the Lord, Trust also in Him, And He shall bring it to pass" (Psalm 37:5). Obedience will require much discipline. We are not perfect; however, we all have the ability to make rational decisions. The Holy Spirit is always present when you enter a compromising situation and are faced with the decision to follow God or please your flesh. That tug that you feel in your spirit is the presence of the Holy Spirit providing the right way for you to turn. Ultimately, when you choose to go the other way, know the blame is solely your responsibility because you failed to obey. Obedience must become a daily decision and a commitment in your life.

Forgiveness is not an option; it is a command. Not only will your burdens be lifted and your faith be strengthened, but most importantly you will finally begin to experience a peace like no other. Only you hold up your freedom experience. ""When Jesus saw their faith, he said, "Friend, your sins are forgiven."" (Luke 5:20, NIV). Just as He did it for me, He will do it for you, too!

Reflections

Reflect on if you struggle with forgiving others. Now list what reasons make forgiveness a challenge in your life.

_____

_____

_____

_____

_____

_____

_____

_____

_____

_____

_____

_____

_____

What steps are you willing to make in order to attain a true spirit of forgiveness? If you feel you have attained this, in what ways can you encourage others to do the same?

_____

_____

_____

_____

_____

_____

_____

_____

_____

_____

_____

_____

_____

_____

Are you currently in a place of in-between faith? If yes, what is causing you to lose faith? If no, what keeps your faith strong?

_____

_____

_____

_____

_____

_____

_____

_____

_____

_____

_____

_____

_____

_____

~ 9 ~
Who to Forgive

So, is that it? Forgiveness spans beyond just the people who have wronged or hurt you. In fact, I believe the main person to forgive is you. Recurring thoughts of "Why do I feel so guilty?" can haunt you for days, months, even years after a negative situation in your life. The feeling of guilt lingers in your spirit even though you did nothing wrong. Often times, you feel guilty thinking you could have responded differently or prevented it somehow. This feeling is like a natural reflex and these thoughts trouble thousands of women each day. You are not alone. We all, on one day or another, have to forgive the person in the mirror. No matter how hard you try to live a good life, trials will come. You will let yourself down and people will not always like you. Learn to overcome your feelings with your faith.

Remember, you are first a spiritual being and it is important that you become skilled at defeating your fears with your faith in the Word. Your earthly body is just a temporary holding cell, but your emotions reside in the spiritual realm. "This is what we speak, not in words taught us by human wisdom but in words taught by the Spirit, explaining spiritual realities with Spirit-taught words. The person without the Spirit does not accept the things that come from the Spirit of God but considers them foolishness, and cannot understand them because they are discerned only through the Spirit. The person with the Spirit makes judgments about all things, but such a person is not subject to merely human judgments..." (1 Corinthians 2:13-15, NIV).

Your feelings block your progress like a dam blocks the natural flow of water. If the water is not properly released, it continues to build and eventually floods. Similarly, your feelings can imprison your ability to move forward and if you never forgive, you become submerged in depression and guilt. But God... Yes, God is your release! God opens the flood gates of your entrapment and all the pain is released over the waterfall so your bruises and wounds may be healed. Think about it. The more water flows, the more it becomes purified. Purify comes from the Latin words *purus* and *ificare* which means clean, cleared, faultless. Therefore, the more you depend on Jesus Christ, the more He will clear your marred memories and make your life faultless. Watch as God transforms your past into a glistening present. Day by day you become more like Him. For His word says, "You shall be holy, for I am holy" (1 Peter 1:16, NASB).

As your life comes and goes, you must learn to forgive ALL those who have hurt you, abused you, cursed you and let you down. This includes you! You see, when someone hurts you, they take power over you. Until you forgive them, they maintain that power. Walk in forgiveness and regain self-control. Know that forgiveness comes from the heart and not from the words you speak. Know that forgiveness shows obedience and through obedience comes freedom!

Stop where you are right now and let's pray: *"Lord Jesus, I love you with all my heart and I want to be free. I ask that you help me as I walk in obedience of your word. Help me to forgive myself and any who have hurt me. I forgive with my heart and not just with my words. Help me to not hold grudges and to not seek revenge, but to sincerely let go. I love you and thank you for my new found freedom in you. In Jesus' mighty name I pray, Amen."*

Reflections

Is there any one you have not been able to forgive? If so, explain why you have been unable to forgive this person(s). Then pray for them and ask God to help you forgive them.

_____

_____

_____

_____

_____

_____

_____

_____

_____

_____

_____

_____

_____

If you prayed the prayer of forgiveness, are you now willing to forgive this person(s) wholeheartedly? If yes, write down their name and what you are forgiving them for. If no, express your struggle.

_____

_____

_____

_____

_____

_____

_____

_____

_____

_____

_____

_____

_____

_____

_____

~ 10 ~
Grace & Mercy

There is nothing greater than God's grace and mercy. His undeserved and uncompromising grace abounds mightily upon your life. In the midst of your storm, God's grace may be an afterthought, but know He is an omnipresent, omniscient, omnipotent God. He's in all places, knows all things and is all powerful!

Let's take a closer look at God's grace. First, God's grace abounds evermore. Grace is God's undeserved favor; giving us what we do not deserve. Let's apply that to everyday life. Think back to day one. What do you really deserve from God? Nothing. Absolutely nothing. But look around. Has not God blessed your life in the midst of your lifestyle? If you are still alive, if you have a job, if you are in good health, if you have food and shelter, if you have access to transportation, if you have a support system, if you wake up every day and get rest every night, you too are a daily recipient of God's grace.

Second, God renews his mercies every day *(Lamentations 3:23, author emphasis).* Mercy is God's compassion when you do wrong; not giving you what you do deserve, but withholding a punishment that is rightly due. It has been established that no one deserves anything from God in the first place. According to God's word, those who participate in homosexuality will not inherit the kingdom of God. That means hell has become your destiny. Death is all you deserve. Be careful not to misinterpret that God is the one who sends you to hell. It is your lack of obedience to God's word and the rejection of the Holy Spirit's guidance that sends you to hell. But God's mercy surrounds you where you are in life right now. He gives each and every person in this world the opportunity to be washed and be made new in Him.

"⁹Do you not know that the unrighteous *and* the wrongdoers will not inherit or have any share in the kingdom of God? Do not be deceived (misled): neither the impure *and* immoral, nor idolaters, nor adulterers, nor those who participate in homosexuality, ¹⁰Nor cheats (swindlers and thieves), nor greedy graspers, nor drunkards, nor foulmouthed revilers *and* slanderers, nor extortioners *and* robbers will inherit or have any share in the kingdom of God. ¹¹And such some of you were [once], But you were washed clean (purified by a complete atonement for sin and made free from the guilt of sin), and you were consecrated (set apart, hallowed), and you were justified [pronounced righteous, by trusting] in the name of the Lord Jesus Christ and in the [Holy] Spirit of our God" (1 Corinthians 6:9-11, AMP).

Think about it. How many times have you passed a policeman while speeding but did not get a ticket? How many times have you been able to park in a close-up space when it was raining outside? How many times have you needed to pay a bill and out of nowhere you found or received the money? All of these instances are prime examples of when God demonstrated His unmerited favor [grace]. And think of how often we fail to thank Him.

Thanking God is another daily commitment that should be a first fruit. First fruit means when God wakes you in the morning the very first thing you do is say "Lord, I thank you."

God freely gives His love, blesses your life with His grace and spares your life with His mercy. He provides a spirit of encouragement when you seek and trust Him and as a result you will begin to experience a greater sense of self-confidence. This is a by-product of God's favor reigning in your life. Without realizing it, you walk with your head higher and a smile on your face. Now it is time to stop and acknowledge the one who has made it all happen. Not just today, but all the time.

The choice is simple and the time is now! Commit to Him. Make the decision to be obedient and He will, without hesitation, give you peace. Thank Him always. "Therefore let us draw near with confidence to the throne of grace, so that we may receive mercy and find grace to help in the time of need" (Hebrews 4:16, NASB).

Reflections

In what ways has God demonstrated His grace and mercy upon your life?

_____

_____

_____

_____

_____

_____

_____

_____

_____

_____

_____

_____

_____

Journal

Use the next few pages as a personal journal. Write down your thoughts and feelings. Reflect on how you felt before and after reading Stage Three.

_____

_____

_____

_____

_____

_____

_____

_____

_____

_____

_____

_____

_____

_____

Stage Four:
FROM BONDAGE to BREAKTHOUGH

"Therefore there is now no condemnation for those who are in Christ Jesus. For the law of the Spirit of life in Christ Jesus has set you free from the law of sin and of death...For the mind set on the flesh is death, but the mind set on the Spirit is life and peace"

(Romans 8: 1-2, 6; NASB)

~ 11 ~
Breaking the Chains

G od truly deserves all the glory each and every day. God—and God alone—will break the chains that have your life entangled. He knew how difficult this life would be; therefore, He sent His only Son to die on Calvary's cross. You see while Jesus hung and died on the cross, His blood was shed for our sins. Yes, Jesus' blood paid for all of our sins. "...for this is My blood of the covenant, which is poured out for many for forgiveness of sins." (Matthew 26:28, NASB) When Jesus paid this debt for us, He paid it in full so that we would never have to worry about it. His death was the ultimate sacrifice. His death has made us free.

Death brings forth life. How so? To die to self is to live in Christ. To die to the flesh is to live in the spirit. You must break the chains that have you bound to your emotional suffering. This bondage brings forth destruction to your mind, body and spirit. But live! Call on the powerful name of Jesus and breakthrough the ruins to a life that promises to bring forth happiness and peace. God has you fully equipped to no longer be bound by fear. You live with greater faith and more self-confidence than ever before. You no longer hold your head down and blame yourself. Instead, walk upright to proclaim that God has healed and delivered you from your afflictions. Your spirit has forgiven and been forgiven. You have been washed and cleansed by the Blood of Jesus. He has brought you to a place of peace.

As you step into this new realm of faith and healing, thank God that the hurt and pain that once had you imprisoned has been loosed. Confront the enemy face to face and exclaim, "You do not have any control over my life! Past destructions are now gone!" The burdens of guilt have been lifted. God has wiped your tears and given you a new smile. Thank Him daily and live this new life striving to make *Him* also smile daily.

You now hold the key to your future. Unlock the cuffs that gripped your life. Unlink the chains that ensnared your mind. Be free from the embarrassment of your circumstances. Stand up boldly. With the sword of the spirit, shatter the chains that confine your entire body. As each link breaks, declare a part of your life free from bondage. Proclaim, "What used to hinder my life, hinders me no more!" Throw away all the hatred, all the distress and all the disgust! Can you feel it? Can you feel the chains breaking? Snatch them off one by one! Call each link by its name...the name that once held you in bondage. Now throw it into the depths of the ocean never to return again.

With all of your renewed strength in God, untie the noose around your neck. Shout with victory that you are alive in Jesus Christ! You survived! What you thought would take you down instead has brought you out! Worship the Lord with all your heart! Praise His mighty and glorious name! Do not hold back the excitement you feel. Give thanks unto Him. As you lift your hands in this breathtaking experience and enter into the presence of God, rejoice! Your day is here, your time is now!

All you feel is relief. Tears of joy stream down your face, chills run through your body and the precious Blood of Jesus Christ cloaks your once-dead spirit. In the most powerful—yet assuring—voice God whispers, "My child, through your obedience comes freedom."

Reflections

What chains have been broken in your life?

_____

_____

_____

_____

_____

_____

_____

_____

_____

_____

_____

_____

_____

_____

Do you now feel alive in Jesus Christ? Share this new feeling.

~ 12 ~
I'm F.R.E.E.

A hhh! What is better than your new found freedom in Jesus Christ? Exhale. Breathe again. Enjoy the soothing in your spirit, the calming in your soul, a peace like no other. Live knowing your dream is fulfilled, your goal achieved, your hope embraced, a reality right here, right now...just for you! This is your season. Walk in your breakthrough! No more sleepless nights, no more tears, and no more pain. Today life reflects love, joy, and peace. Not only has God called you out of darkness and into His marvelous light, but most importantly you are His friend.

Together, you have broken through the glass ceiling of homosexuality. You no longer look up and wonder what life would be like on the other side. Instead, you stand in awe and thank God for what your life has become. No more looking back. Only look forward in anticipation and great expectation of God's promises for your life. You were chosen before the Earth was formed, accepted as His beloved child, redeemed by His bloodshed, informed about His will, given an inheritance according to His purpose and sealed with the

Holy Spirit of promise. (Ephesians 1:4-14, *author emphasis*). All of these things God did for you. Now as you hear His word, rest in Him.

As you continue to enjoy this uplifting experience, realize you are now at a new level in Jesus Christ. You are victorious and not defeated. God has seen your determination and your heart to trust Him. Your prayers have been answered and your self-worth restored. God's favor is reigning over your life. From this day, resist the devil. You are a new person! "After you have suffered for a little while, the God of all grace, who called you to His eternal glory in Christ, will Himself perfect, confirm, strengthen *and* establish you" (1 Peter 5:10, NASB).

Your soul is purified and your mind is clear. Your walk is new and you love with a pure heart. Begin each day thanking God for your breakthrough. At all times, keep Him first. Be happy knowing you now get to spend your eternity with Jesus Christ. Celebrate life and be glad. Your obedience has made you free so prepare to live in the peace of the Lord. You are free. You are free. You are free! **Forever Rejoice and Enjoy Eternity!**

Reflections

As you celebrate being F.R.E.E., what promises do you trust God to fulfill in your new life?

_____

_____

_____

_____

_____

_____

_____

_____

_____

_____

** Right now, take just a moment to spend with the Lord. Embrace His presence.

Express your love for Him. Thank Him for His goodness. Enjoy your Friend! **

~ 13 ~
The Next Day

The power of God's deliverance is real. You will not wonder if it really happened. You will feel a distinct change in your heart with respect to that particular lifestyle or habit. You will not have the same urges to do what you use to do, and it is a crystal-clear change in your mindset and the way you now desire to live your life.

Do not confuse this with never making a mistake or sinning again. My deliverance was a move of God. It wasn't a grandioso church service or a weekend revival where the preacher called me by name and laid hands on me. God spoke to me right in my living room...just me, my dog and God. There was no question in my heart or mind that He had heard my cry and that day was my appointed time. It was in that serene moment that my mind was made up that I would no longer live as a lesbian because God had not created me that way. Psalms 139:14 confirms that I am fearfully and wonderfully made. I was created in His own image (author emphasis, Genesis 1:27.) I knew in that moment my life would never be the same.

So what do I do now? I've prayed, I've cried, God has delivered me, I've rested and the next day is here. What do I do now? I am a firm believer that God performs miracles in today's time. I have witnessed a young lady be delivered from smoking and never turn back. I mean not even the slightest temptation. Sometimes when God moves the temptation is 100% taken away right then and there. It is like amnesia, a memory lost forever like it never happened in your life. In this case, all the desires are erased. There are other times when a person can experience the delivering power of God, but in the days ahead as your process manifests, you may still encounter temptation from the enemy. This is what happened in my life and every day I chose to make a conscious decision to make God smile. Yes my life had changed, yes my mind was new, yes my heart was not the same, but homosexuality seemed to be more present around me now more than ever before.

I have not read one scripture that says deliverance is the total absence of temptation. "No temptation has overtaken you except such as is common to man; but God is faithful, who will not allow you to be tempted beyond what you are able, but with the temptation will also make the way of escape, that you may be able to bear it. (1 Corinthians 10:13) "Seeing then that we have a great High Priest who has passed through the heavens, Jesus the Son of God, let us hold fast our confession. For we do not have a High Priest who cannot sympathize with our weaknesses, but was in all points tempted as we are, yet without sin. Let us therefore come boldly to the throne of grace, that we may obtain mercy and find grace to help in time of need." (Hebrews 4: 14-16) Instead, the scriptures reminds us that during this process when temptation may come, God will equip us through his son Jesus with grace to endure these trying times.

As I began to share my story, I kept it real with other women I met because my transition was not easy. I found myself being tested by the enemy every single day. I was ridiculed by many as a sellout. I was told I was brainwashed. I was criticized for not being true to myself. I was even told because I didn't wear dresses more often now I was just talk. And yes some days all this negativity made me want to question my life, but I realized people judge you when they don't know your truth. I am not a people pleaser and my clothes do not identify me. As long as my daily walk and talk reflect the God who lives within me, my life is and will be a living testimony. The devil was angry that I found the truth in God's word about my identity in Christ. I was no longer living a life of sin and I wanted to share my testimony with other women so they too would have the opportunity to experience the love of Christ and be free in Him.

But the devil was not having that. He constantly tried to convince my mind that God had let me down because I still had some personal issues. Even though I was not attracted to women, my spirit was being penetrated with other unhealthy desires. The enemy tried to destroy my mind with other desires like pornography and disobedience. In the midnight hour, I found myself trying to justify these sins thinking it was better than being a lesbian. I found myself desiring the urge to drink again and my mouth was foul. I often times would be upset with myself because I was confused on why these bad habits had returned. I felt like God had delivered me from my alternative lifestyle, but maybe the enemy was right in that God did not love me enough to deliver me from all my struggles. Lie, lie, lie! The Holy Spirit quickened my spirit and reminded me that there is no level of sin and condemnation. I am to live holy and obey God in ALL areas of my life. I must repent daily and live as a disciple of Christ.

Remember, it took me almost 18 months after my prayer of deliverance to finally die to my flesh and fully surrender to God. He was patiently waiting on me. God knew until I was completely ready to let all of my fleshly desires go and live in the fruits of the spirit, He could not move forward in my purpose and destiny. As you read this book today, I walk in total deliverance and freedom from an alternative lifestyle, sexual perversion, alcohol and the words from my mouth speak life. Am I perfect? No but I try to live every second of every day of my life as a disciple of Christ so people can see Him in me. For me, it only takes that moment to reflect on the goodness of God and remember the tears of joy I shed that day in my living room. No matter what anyone else says to me or thinks about me I am not and will never be the woman I use to be.

Don't be discouraged if your life actions and reactions do not change instantaneously. Know that with a sincere spirit and prayer for deliverance, God will change your heart and mind. For you, like me, the process of dying to your flesh, however, may be the gradual process. I have heard some people try to argue that God's deliverance is not a process and if it does not happen immediately it is not of God. I boldly believe it depends on God's purpose in that particular person's circumstances. My deliverance was without a doubt a process but in the end His dominion reigns supreme in my life. In fact, how could this chapter have even been written without the process!

My heart's prayer is that God will use my testimony to touch and change lives. I live to see others set free! This book was not just written for the person struggling with sexual identity. This book is also for those living in the life, unsure about the life, confused in the life, parents with a child in the life, the friend of someone in the life, the pastor with a member in the life. Trust me I understand, even though it shouldn't, the perspective changes when you are faced with homosexuality under your own roof versus just someone you know. This does not change our responsibility as Christians regardless of who the person is. For example, many churches offer support for recovering alcoholics, drug addicts and those abused from domestic violence. We, the church, must also begin to support those who struggle with homosexuality.

Be clear in what I am saying! Not all those who are living a homosexual life desire to know or live by the Word of God. Deliverance is a choice! It was not until I began to read God's word for myself that I realized the life I was living was not the life God had destined for me to live as a woman. It was only in that personal realization that my heart desired to be delivered and set free. From that point, God worked on me, in me and through me to get me where I am today. I am a woman free of homosexuality fighting this generational curse on my bloodline so it bounds no one else!

I leave you with this. No matter what you are going through, if you seek Him, God will work on your behalf. If you have been through and brought out of anything in your life, God has delivered you. If you have been delivered by the Blood of Jesus, you have changed closets. If you have changed closets, then let's pray for someone else. Never be ashamed to share your testimony because you may be the key to someone else's jumpstart to freedom and Trading Closets.

Journal

Use the next few pages as a personal journal. Write down your thoughts and feelings. Reflect on God's delivering power and how you will live the next day and days to come.

_____

_____

_____

_____

_____

_____

_____

_____

_____

_____

_____

_____

_____

Resources

National Suicide Prevention Lifeline
1-800-273-TALK (1-800-273-8255)

National Hopeline Network
1-800-SUICIDE (1-800-784-2433)

National Drug & Alcohol Treatment Hotline
1-800-662-HELP (1-800-662-4357)

www.ingramcontent.com/pod-product-compliance
Lightning Source LLC
Chambersburg PA
CBHW072041040426
42447CB00012BB/2964